Speed Of Dark

Poems by
Julia Vinograd

Art by Deborah Vinograd

Zeitgeist Press

cover photo: Harold Parrish
art: Deborah Vinograd

ISBN: 0-929730-58-5

Zeitgeist Press
1630 University Avenue #34
Berkeley, CA 94703 U.S.A.

CONTENTS

PEOPLE WITH NOWHERE TO GO ON THANKSGIVING

On thanksgiving Lonely cooks and eats
the people with nowhere to go.
I've seen them stuffed with screams
like chestnut turkey stuffing broiling on street corners.
A slow broil.
Or in rooms where the tv shows them
endless pictures of happy family gatherings;
Lonely eats thanksgiving tvs like candied yams.
Lonely's a good cook, he's learned
if he puts in too much despair they can't feel it.
But they can be stewed in liquor
and still not get drunk enough to forget.
Thanksgiving's a special meal,
he uses his best black linen tablecloth
and sharp knives made of old thanksgiving memories
when there was somewhere to go.
Lonely even says grace,
folding his long cold hands
and praising the abundance gathered before him.

WOMAN ON THE BUS

She's wearing a neon green and orange
horizontal-striped polyester pants suit
and she's so fat she has to sit
with her thighs wide apart to support her tummy.
She takes up 2 bus spaces,
much to the disgust of the little old man
crammed in next to her like a withered pretzel
about to snap. She's as old as he is
under her hennaed red hair and thick greasy lipstick.
Her neck is one solid bulge
from where her chin should be
to a little over the collar of her pants suit.
Bright cheap plastic bracelets
clatter desperately at her wrists
trying to get away from her.
The toenails of her varicose veined sandaled feet
are painted orange to match her pants suit
and there's a small straw hat perched uneasily
on her big hair, its orange ribbon
studded with smile buttons.
No one can look that awful without effort,
it's deliberate.
She doesn't slump and may even be smiling.
Her clever eyes are buried behind rolls of fat
like weasels hiding in a hedge.
There's a romance novel sticking out of her shoulder bag.
And there's more than one way of getting even.

ON THE ASSASSINATION OF ISRAELI PRIME MINISTER RABIN

This is the end of a day
as they count eternal days.
Everyone in the Mideast is always right,
everyone in the Mideast is always wrong.
That hasn't changed.
But if all the dead heroes were sitting in deck chairs
staring over the dead sea
and talking as the spirit moves them,
today polite attendants would start taking down
the striped umbrellas
and closing the concession stands
and even bringing out a rack to pile the deck chairs on
though they'd never dare ask the dead heroes to get up.
We never killed one of our own before,
there were always enough other people to kill us,
a day has ended.
It's not as if I paid attention,
to me he was only an important suit;
I vaguely agreed with him without listening much.
But I know if the dead heroes stop watching the dead sea
and go in for the night
night will fall.
And in that night sand will blow
covering the cities, burying the cities.
Sand that acknowledges neither god nor man.

LAUGH TRACKS

I complained to a friend about laugh tracks on television
and he told me they did a study and proved
people are afraid to laugh alone.
Crying alone is very popular,
look at the afternoon soaps.
Also fear, suspense is heightened by wondering
what's behind every creak in the hall
and being scared to get up and turn on the light.
But laughter's dangerous, madmen laugh alone.
You hear your own voice laughing,
you might hear something underneath it,
you don't want to know.
The canned laugh tracks drown it all out.
Feelgood tracks.
I have junky friends with feelgood tracks
to drown it all out. It works.
But why? We're proud when we make a child laugh
as if we'd made the sun come out
and we set ourselves above the animals
because we laugh.
So are we only animals in lonely rooms
watching a glowing box and imitating strange sounds,
tossing them out of our throats
as a seal tosses a ball on its nose?
Do we trust laugh tracks to keep track of us
and protect us from being human?
Canned laughter for people who can't
or can we?
Why are we scared to be human?
Why are we scared to be us?

ON THE ROAD

On the highway, on the lowway
driving like a child with a coloring book,
stay inside the white line
as all the colors wear down
under your thumb, under your eyelids,
under your wheels.
On the lowway to nowhere the moon howls
and a trainwhistle howls back,
you're not stopping for either of them.
The steering wheel grips your wrists
till the bones are raw.
There'll be an all night diner
in the town coming up
but first get that seatbelt on your tongue.
Your mind isn't safe.
On the highway the sky falls in the way,
slices of blue sharp enough to puncture your wheels,
dissolving in the rear-view mirror to rain.
Just as if you weren't driving.
The lowway knows you can't believe your eyes.
It shows everything, blatantly,
dancing gods and old flames' faces.
You ignore it all.
You grit your teeth and look only
for the turn off to that all-night diner
with its strong coffee and congealed potatoes.

BROKEN PROMISES

I knew a man who kept a flock of broken promises
in cages on the roof of his building in the slums.
His landlord told him pets were forbidden
but the man said they weren't pets
and if the landlord bothered him again
he'd let them out.
The broken promises made ugly, nagging squawks,
but they didn't look scary, not locked up.
The man looked scary.
He looked at the landlord and the landlord went away.
The man wore heavy gloves
to stroke their curved beaks.
He remembered the curve of a woman's breasts
and his hands clenched inside the gloves.
The broken promises did not have broken wings,
they beat against the rusted bars,
their eyes slitting, trying to get out.
The man stared back with a yellow grin,
haunted, vicious, stubborn.
This was how he kept his promises
in cages on the roof of his building in the slums.
And yes, they hurt him
and no, he wouldn't let them go.

6

PEARLS

I was watching figureskating championships on tv,
sparkling costumes spinning in mid air,
colored lights, standing ovations,
a mere breath off was fatal.
Then something happened and I could see thru the ice;
it wasn't a sports rink anymore,
it was the sea full of drowned people.
Some of them floated so close to the surface
that blades of ice skates went over their limp necks.
Schools of semi-transparent fish swam thru their hair
and nibbled their fingers.
It was too dark to see how many there were
or how long they'd been dead.
All the lights were on the young girl
doing a double axel.
Waves made their hands look
as if they were still reaching upwards for help.
A second later and it was gone
and I was watching a commercial for breakfast cereal
as if it were interesting.
I turned down the sound.
I decided I hadn't seen anything.
People die all the time, but what can I do?
Besides, they were already dead.
When the figureskating came back on
I knew I wouldn't see anything more
and I didn't.
But the first skater was wearing a pearl choker.
Real matched pearls from the depths of the sea.

WAR

War walks thru the streets touching no one yet.
He keeps his hands in his pockets
and his eyes dart out from under a baseball cap
occasionally. Appraising.
There's a corner flowerstand,
he's always liked flowers,
all those cemeteries.
He sends a private smile to wrap around the roses
crinkly as cellophane.
There are troops in yesterday's newspaper
and they may be crumpled and thrown away
like yesterday's newspaper.
War isn't thinking of them, not yet.
He looks like any other run-away,
thin, not to be trusted, an explosion of nerves
and cold hands.
Mouth warm as the muzzle of a just fired gun.
The streets do not collapse in smoke behind him,
there are no purple trees of screams.
War whistles under his breath, feeling his way.
Staggering street guys collect plastic bags
of squashed tin cans,
spiders collect drained flies.
War has his own collection:
The glamour of heroes larger than life
because they're not alive any more.
Medals of extreme valour. Meals ready to eat.
Marching songs.
Fingerprints falling like snowflakes,
no two alike.
But time has to break around his wrist
where we have a pulse, and war has us.
It's important to him

to know what it all looked like before.
Streetcleaners in the morning rain.
Shopwindows spilling treasure chests of costume jewelry.
Secretaries pulling up their blinds
in badly heated rooms
and stirring the mirror like stew.
Highheels rattling past like machineguns.
War studies everything almost gently.
He waits.

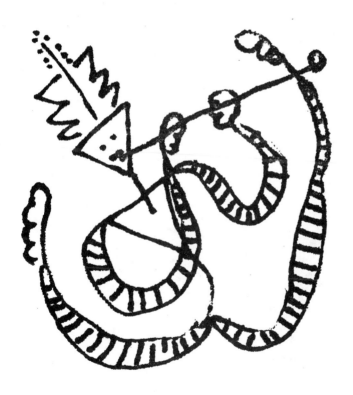

DEADHEADS

I remember deadheads coming up to me
while I was having coffee in the med
and saying "You don't know us
but we were rolling joints on your face
thru 2 states on the way to the show,
it was a great show."
That's one way to have a famous book.
I hadn't planned the cover
to be just the right size
and they hadn't planned to wind up reading poems.
Fair enough.
And I'd usually trade a book for their beaded earrings
or shiny anklets.
I felt like I was selling America
back to the Indians.
Deadheads wore roses, Indians wore feathers,
both followed visions.
Money was kept strictly for tickets and gasoline.
What would I have seen if I could've looked
out of all my eyes on all the copies of my book?
Luck of the road. And now, gone.

FIERCE OLD WOMEN

There's an army of fierce old women with glasses,
bad teeth and swollen ankles
defending a sandcastle from the sea.
They're shuffled from busy relatives to cheap rooms
to nursing beds as their white hair foams.
Home is a set of yellowed photographs
pasted on the walls of a sandcastle.
A child playing on the same beach with a red pail
digs up a crystal from a chandelier
that lit a long ago dance.
They don't have a chance.
They're gone and no one wants them back.
Fierce old women have knitting needles
to stab the sea,
and arthritis twisted as coral
and clean print dresses washed in tears
salt as the deep. They don't sleep much anymore.
They fight for every grain of sand,
for every wattled layer of throat
and lump of skin.
The tide's coming in.
Thin-lipped, they clutch an umbrella or a purse.
If they're caught in a hospital their hands clench air.
The sand stairs crumble,
then the tower and the hour.
Fierce old women.
I watch them and I smell the sea.

BLUES

I've had the blues for lost lovers
and I know what to do with those blues:
hurt and crash and burn
and then return you to our regular program.
Loss costs a lot but living costs more
and it's got to be got.
Nothing's forgotten,
not a freckled collarbone
or a slammed door,
but the world doesn't have the decency to end.
I've got the lost love blues in bottles
down in my cellar,
ageing like purple wine for lonely winter nights.
I thought I knew the blues, but what's to do
when I look around and find
I've lost myself?
Don't know how it happened.
My eyes see the world which still hasn't ended.
Bent light flickers over my shoes.
There's blues where I used to be,
but they're not my blues.
And I don't know what happens now.

PRAYER

We're expected to wear
the sort of clothes to visit god
that we'd wear to visit a maiden aunt.
And be on the same kind of good behavior.
As if a leap of faith were taken on tip-toe
in shiny too-tight shoes.
As if anything could shock god. How silly.
I'd rather roll and rootle in the stars
like a pig in mud, grunting, glad, feeding.
The guzzling spirit has no limits;
god has no table manners.
I'd rather be packed naked in wormy ooze
with all the dead and all the living
going up in god's wildfire voice.
Our names ring like bells, big, brassy,
breaking the sky.
I don't want an answer as if I were scoring the world
on a high school test.
I want to be wrenched open, savaged,
have the world's screaming horrors and beauty
thrust down my throat with both hands.
Dying soldiers calling for help
after the battle's passed them.
Children's jump-rope songs. Unemployment lines.
Lovers. Small green leaves.
I don't want to understand,
I don't think it's possible.
I want to be turned into an answer.

OLD GUNSLINGER

The many different colors in the rock
he was hiding behind when someone shot at him
and how cold it felt against his skin.
He remembered that.
Went back looking for the rock when everyone was dead,
couldn't find it.
Wondered if he'd ever see anything that clearly again
but couldn't figure out why it mattered.
It was just a rock.
Not very pretty or remotely valuable.
He didn't drink because drinkers talk
and everything he thought about was like that rock,
it didn't even make sense to him.
He didn't remember the men he killed
or the men who tried to kill him.
His gun had no surprises, he knew it too well.
A field of some bright yellow wildflower
with heavy pollen,
brushing it off himself afterwards
he was more embarrassed than he ever was by blood.
It clung, and the scent lasted for days.
He had less trouble with women.
Things he only noticed
because his mind kept going back to them.
The absolute shock of snow-melted water
he'd had to jump in once,
he'd wanted to yell though of course he couldn't.
The water wanted him to yell.
He always checked what snuck up
from the corners of his eyes
or he would've been dead years ago.
But he felt these little things that couldn't hurt him
sneaking up from the corners of his mind.
And he wondered what to do about them.

A BONE PEN

Today a friend gave me a pen
made of a hollow smooth bone,
a knob at each end and the curved length
very strokable.
So I could hold all of death between my thumb
and fingers when I write.
Medicine men use bones, sometimes to cure.
Today I also went for a flue shot
in a fluorescent-lit hospital
where I signed a blurred yellow form
and they came up behind my left shoulder.
I never saw the needle.
Bones and needles. Medicine.
Visions and secrets. Doctors use needles,
sometimes to cure.
But there are enough dry bones in the world.
Graveyards. Battlefields.
And I wouldn't have died of the flue,
I'd just wish I were dead.
But not having the flu is also not enough.
What I want to hold
between my thumb and fingers when I write
is all of life.

15

DOES TELEVISION MAKE US MORE VIOLENT?

Probably less.
When a guy with 2 kids loses his job
to someone working part-time at half pay
and his medical insurance came with the job
and the baby's coughing all night
he already wants to kill.
Either the guy who fired him
or the guy who stole his job
or anyone in the building
where they all smiled at him every morning for years
and then cut his throat.
He has 3 choices.
Either go down with a machine gun
and take as many as he can with him.
(Some do, it makes the news.)
Or beat on his family
because he has to hit someone
and he can't stand their pity,
it makes him feel dirty.
(Many do, it doesn't make the news.)
Or turn on the tv and watch Dirty Harry
do his killings for him. Or Rocky.
Or the Terminator. He isn't thinking of actors.
The deaths are real to him, they have to be.
Death is in him and it has to go somewhere.
If Jesus died in our place
the television kills in our place.
With lots of blood and screams.
If violence is legislated out of television
and the only programs are warm and fuzzy
there could be more killings.
Because death is in us all
and it has to go somewhere.

24 HOUR DONUT SHOP

I haven't thought of the 24 hour donut shop in years.
I'd pass by it at night
and glance at all those people
twitching symphonically
as if they'd fallen into those chairs
from 12 story windows and weren't even dead.
More telepathically uninterested.
I never saw anyone actually eat
any of the congealing donuts.
Coffee yes, but more to warm the hands.
These are fingers, remember fingers?
It wasn't exactly scary,
it was more an intermission from outer space.
And the one rule, the sign that rose over that place
like a private moon, the sign that said:
"No Talking To Invisible People".
The management didn't *care* what was real.
Invisible people could stay
as long as they stayed quiet.
Sometimes when I passed the 24 hour donut shop
I could see the invisible people better
than the remains of customers.
But I didn't talk to them either.
I still followed rules, pretty much from habit.
I was too young to know I was young.

PORTRAIT

He's 19 and glows in the dark;
from here on it's all downhill.
His only wish is to be wished on
like a falling star.
Homes are only tv settings
to advertise instant coffee,
mouth wash and vacuum cleaners.
He lives in a cleaner vacuum,
couch-surfing an ocean of breaking beds.
He balances his body against all expectations
as nightflesh crashes and sobs against his skin.
He doesn't care enough to be unkind;
he's even vaguely sorry for everyone
who isn't him.
Lately he's been telling each new person
a different life story, so when he dies young
or the world ends he'll have memories.
witnessed and believed in.
He loses his own life as it happens,
surfers don't remember names of waves.
Rich-and-famous is a consolation prize
for people who can't get into nightclubs on their looks.
Why should he live as if there were a future?
A future is for people left out now,
planning to get even.
Couch-surfers wipe out, falling stars crash and burn.
He knows, it doesn't matter.
Look at him, thin wrist raised to the curl of his mouth.
Make a wish.

MOURNER

A mourner with a knife in a forest clearing
duelling with the slanted light,
leaping in and out of the sun.
Bunched muscles tense and furious tears
run unheeded. I don't know who died.
But nothing can be the same again,
the sky will wear scars if he's fast enough.
The moist new leaves curl away from him,
hiding their faces in wind.
Total silence.
Bare feet muffled in moss.
His throat looks as if he's swallowed a stone.
He's not fighting to win,
the dead stay dead.
But things have no right to go on
as if nothing happened,
he's got a knife that says so.

LOITERER

He hides in a tarot deck when the cops come by.
They don't want him,
but they also don't want him around.
He hides under the Magician's table
and steals some wine from the cup
(there's a price for that wine
but he'd pay it anyway).
Or he hides in hell behind the cardboard flames,
sticking out a grubby, sparechanging hand
to whoever's fortune is being read.
Nobody sees. Nobody ever sees.
He knows why the world ended
and anyone who says it's still going on
is just slow.
They'll learn.
He doesn't talk to himself anymore,
he got tired of listening.
He's got a habit of clutching his skinny elbows hard
as if his whole body might blow apart
like a tumbleweed in a dust storm.
I've seen him at the bottom of the Fool's cliff
arguing which one of them should jump.
He gets around.
He smells of shadows, dogs don't like him.
He swam thru a bubbling marsh of cement
before it became a city.
His fingerprints are underfoot forever.

GUNS

On tv a politician worked himself up,
jowls quivering, tie askew
over "guns out there in the night,
hunting honest citizens, men with guns."
And it sounded like the men
were almost an afterthought.
I imagined guns shaking their tired owners awake
cold barrels gleaming in the cold dawn,
guns eager to go out and kill
while their owners plead weakly
"at least let me have some breakfast first."   .
I imagine guns leaping into holsters and saying
"ya gotta feed me first, now giddyap."
As if guns ride men out hunting
the way men ride horses, spurs against sides
that would rather see eggs over easy than blood.
But guns shout and blood comes.
The gun whips its man away,
clambering over wall and roofs.
The gun runs with his legs and praises the man,
they'll be together always.
Men stabled by their guns
in cheap anonymous hotel rooms
where guns that never sleep
watch their wistful dreams contemptuously.
Men dream of gentle laughing women
in flowered dresses,
what a waste of time, their guns snap.
Guns that own men the way men own horses.
Guns that command "now hurry up, we're going hunting,
can't you shave later, I waited all night for this,
I'm hungry."

VILLAGE MUSIC

A cry in the throat gargling sorrow
like cold water. Can't stop.
Men of the village dance on gravestones,
bitterly alive in winter.
Loose black clothes with red scarves, red sashes. Snow.
Women pour out wine and honey on the graves
and watch the earth, saying nothing.
A column of vibrating air
with a bristling greybeard attached
chanting. Not a funeral.
They're feeding their dead because the cattle are sick,
it'll be hard to feed the living this year.
Their breath ghosts in air, the only ghosts.
Urgently lost music, mostly strings,
like falling down a flight of stairs
faster and faster. Can't stop.
Dancing can't stop or hunger.
Honey and wine in red clay bottles
for the dead who stopped.
Because there was none to spare
and now there's even less.
The living leave proud
following the fiddles back to their cows
with sad heaving sides who don't understand.

MORNING FOG

Heavy morning fog thick as a murder mystery
in an old movie.
Whoever's following me can get very close.
Whoever's following you can get very close.
Would you like to be followed?
Would you like to be the only source of light
to a lover or a mugger?
The fog's a white dustcloth over buildings
as over old furniture abandoned in an attic;
the rest of the world doesn't matter.
Whoever's following me waits in a doorway
tasting my exhaled breath as I pass,
as an appetizer.
Whoever's following you regrets the anonymous gloves,
your skin is warm.
In fog we are followed.
In fog we follow.
What doorway are you standing in, silently waiting?
Who are you waiting for?

23

GHOSTS

In ancient savage times people were sacrificed
at the building of a temple
so their ghosts would protect it.
The first stone was laid where the heart used to be.
In modern savage times
nobody's sure where the heart is.
He was drunk and strangled her
to stop her screaming,
now he's trying to shake her back to life.
He's crying.
The machine gun keeps shooting,
making the corpse twitch,
it won't stop until it's empty.
Police don't question stone walls,
only people imitating them.
In modern savage times
even ghosts are on the take,
they do not protect and serve.

SITTING

One of my favorite pictures was of a fierce old king
in a black throne with 2 panthers crouched by him.
And I'm sitting on a public bench
where the streets divide
and 2 buses just roared by me,
one on either side.
I can feel the king's cold fingers
grasping the embroidered velvet
and the children in the bus
grasping at the cord
to make the bus stop.
To make time stop.
And nothing stops, nothing at all.

HORN ON THE STREET

A horn moans and shudders,
writhing like a snake shedding its skin,
music groans bright as blood.
Nobody calls a doctor or even stops
to catch the spilling sounds.
They might be contagious.
They're definitely not insured.
The musician crouched behind his horn
has nowhere to go for the night.
The night crouched behind the musician
has nowhere to go.
"Go away fast as love has gone," the song says
"before night follows you home.
Better not get involved."
The musician crouched behind his horn
hasn't eaten for so long his stomach's shrunk,
he's forgotten he's hungry.
But the night crunched behind the musician
licks its lips. Slowly. Smiling.
The horn plays a pet name
you haven't been called in so long.
"Go away fast as love has gone," the song says
"you can't be helped anymore."

RIVER

Dark water. A half-rotted branch
dislodges a dead hand.
There must've been a battle.
A few guns sank to the bottom, silt-clogged, silent.
A toad makes loud victorious toad noises
and lilies don't argue.
Thin silver fish shake blood from their gills indignantly,
the water's beginning to clear.
The armies marched on as best they could.
Dark water out of reach.
A few feet away a man who knows he's dying
tries to remember his girl
but all he sees is water.
Dark cool water he'll never drink.

THE DOOR THAT SWUNG OPEN BEHIND ME

The door that swung open behind me
wasn't there when I turned around.
When I turned back everything looked the same,
I'd always spoken this language, hadn't I?
Streets spun from the palm of my hand
like a spool of bright colored crepe paper
and I knew them all
as well as I knew the palm of my hand
but hadn't I been left-handed?
The door that swung open behind me
didn't creak or let in a slant of light
like a sword over my shoulder
or do any of the "I am a door" things
I'd seen in the movies.
When I turned around I couldn't remember
what I was looking for
and when I turned back my memories
had someone else's fingerprints.
The sky was the color the sky always was
at this hour, I had the name for the color
but it hurt my mouth like sour apples.
The door that swung open behind me
was a blank wall of faded bricks
when I turned around.
We looked at each other for a moment
until the wall asked me
"Well? Are you a door?"

QUARREL

I don't like quarrels and not because
I'm particularly fond of people.
But I'm not speaking to someone at the moment
which means he's got a chainsaw of silence
for the chip on my shoulder
and I've got a chainsaw of silence
for the chip on his shoulder
and between the 2 of us
I can't hear the espresso machine blasting off
or the ceiling playing gently bottled jazz
or any other sweet unnatural noise of the city.
Annoying. Like when cable reception goes out
because a squirrel fried itself on the wires.
He is a bit like a chittering squirrel
and I'm trying to fast-forward
to when I'll be vaguely sorry he doesn't exist
but much more pleased that my machine's working again.
For me quarrels have very little to do
with the person involved.
But it's so much trouble to get the air started up,
to get a handle on the wind.
Where's the pliers I used on the constellations
last time, and why is there a plastic replica
of Old MacDonald's Farm all over my best toolbox?
No, I don't like quarrels.

YOUNG GIRL

Her clothes catch fire from her skin.
That dark green silk respectable blouse
flashes and flakes to grey ash in one breath
while her soft breasts
are trying to carry on an ordinary conversation.
Sparks blow out of her black linen trousers,
tearing the seams. She doesn't notice.
She's still nibbling the damp end
of a long dark curl, frowning a little.
Nobody warned her new moons rise in her fingernails
to eclipse the sun.
She's probably got a name, most people do
but the fire doesn't.
She's sitting at an outdoor cafe table
enamelled in winter sunlight
with politely crossed knees
as the fire roars into microphones
and burns up reporters.
Her wristwatch had a heart-attack
from being too close to her pulse,
it was a cheap watch, she wasn't surprised.
She has no idea.
The line of her throat saying nothing
and the stabbing wail of fire engines.
Hoses and ladders and red shiny coats,
as if anything could help.

MINE

A child builds a town with colored blocks.
"This is the post office where I get my mail,
this is the school, this is the movie theatre,
the parks inside here, these toothpicks are trees
and in summer they'll have all the fruits at once.
This blue block is a lake, there're shells
at the bottom of it.
This block with gold stars is the candystore,
I go there everyday.
This is my town, I can knock it down
when I want to. All the houses are mine.
I change rooms like clothes, this one is spanish,
this one's a skyscraper, this one's a cottage
with rose vines over it.
No, nobody else lives here. Why should they?
They can get their own colored blocks."

STORM

Lightning all over fast, like a giant flashbulb
taking a mug shot of the cowering city
and all the power's gone.
My nice warm apartment where people had problems on tv
is gone, and I've fallen into a dark cave.
If I reach my hands in front of my face
I can separate black outlines from other blackness.
Windows rattle, the light kept them from breaking,
only the light.
I move my hands and feet like a bear, slowly,
trying to ward off snarling little tables
that leap at my knees.
The tv is just another rock.
Food goes bad in the ice box, besides as a bear
I should hunt my own food. Lumbering. Patient.
Blankets still warm. Heavy and furry.
When I go out into streets without traffic lights
the wilderness will have grown back.
Rain pounding on rainforests.
Trees 4 foot across at the base and disappearing upwards.
Giant nameless fish I scoop out of a churning river
and bring wriggling to my mouth with my paws.

CIRCUS

I didn't see a circus, not exactly.
The lovely bareback rider
somersaulting from her white horse
is cut in half
by the wide-brimmed hat of the fat woman
who sat in front of me.
Cut in half more surely than any magician
with a saw and a lady in a velvet-draped box.
Even binoculars can't reach the acrobats,
there's a dazzling knot of spangles and limbs
too high to see.
I crane my neck and squint into the spotlight,
trying not to breathe in case it distracts them.
I only know the high wire's there
because they haven't fallen. Yet.
When the lion trainer kneels in front of the lion
with a flourish and commands
I can't see inside the lion's mouth with him
as those curved teeth raise over his neck
but I also can't see anything else,
I almost feel that rank meaty breath over my face.
I didn't see a circus, I was a circus.
And what I remember is what I didn't see.
Too bright, too scary, and it all happened too fast.
Like love. Eyes closed to remember the dark.

STREET MUSICIAN

Electric guitar on the street.
Long greasy hair whipped over his grin.
Camouflage shirt, spare a war?
Heavy veined arms strangle his instrument
thumbs first. It yells and gulps for air.
He stamps a boot down as if a creeping arm
were grasping for his ankle.
And he throws his body over the baby amplifier
as a grenade lands.
Guitar strings stretched over an explosion.
About 25. Relishing every stolen breath
between his teeth.
He's got the goodlooks that only come
from not being dead.
Every day the music dies in his place
under his angry hands.

FLEA MARKET RAP

"This bone fell out of a bag of bones
Georgia O'Keeffe was bringing home
from the desert, she didn't notice,
she never got to paint it, it can be yours.
Feel how smooth, how full of shining death.
And it's not *that* badly broken,
if you're handy you could fix it up
so even its previous owner wouldn't notice.
Or come christmas season you could carve it up
and make hash pipes to sell to the tourists.
People love the way smoke stains bone.
Make your fortune, easy.
If you look ahead, it's an investment really,
like investment banking.
Or just keep it on your desk, almost casual,
the way the old guys did with human skulls.
Think big thoughts and impress the girls.
Who can resist?"

35

STUDENTS

Already half-digested by diagrams,
only their kicking feet dangle
from the theoretical monster's mouth.
Prove the theory and the monster
will applaud your taste.
There's no escape.
Heroes are no match for homework.
The bad breath of dead people's love lives,
the sharp teeth of tests,
being tied to your desk by an outline
while everyone else goes out to party.
I've seen students in the coffeehouse
with that stunned look.
They've been kicked in the face by footnotes.
They've been hit by a semi-truck of statistics
and they're breathing very carefully
in case there's internal bleeding.
They look at the chocolate rum cake
from such a long distance.
They remember when it tasted good.

THE CITY

The city wears a tight black dress with huge red roses
grasping at her like rude sweaty hands.
The petals are callused. Roses that work
in factories, on the docks, drunken roses
with red swollen faces. Rage. Heat.
Children wailing. Roses that throw themselves
like handgrenades against her cool hips.
The city goes to the finest restaurants
but her dress is too tight for her to eat.
Hungry hands reach from the roses to steaming roasts
but silken stitches tie the hands.
Strangle the screams.
The food is thrown away.
The city wonders if she'll have to use make-up
to hide the roses' bruises again.
No one is satisfied.
And she doesn't tip well either.

WAKE

I found myself unexpectedly at a wake tonight
at a bar for one of the regulars.
They did it right, in 5 minutes I felt
we were doing it right
and I hadn't known the guy.
His widow asked his favorite band
and led the dancing, her face fierce,
her body spinning.
I was connected to everyone in the room,
the dead man's blood danced in all our veins.
I wonder what he looked like.
The band made the floorboards live,
the cold cement warehouse live,
it even made us live the way living ought to be.
Our skins steamed.
I thought of the Aztecs. The Druids.
Are we only really alive when someone dies?
Suppose it had nothing to do with sin
and Jesus died so we could party.
Suppose the gods are only bright piñatas
to be beaten, broken open, with gifts inside.
Why must we imitate them?
I never met the guy.
I loved him tonight, I loved us all tonight.
But I wish I could believe
I'd love him better alive.

HALLOWEEN MASK

I saw my own face hanging in a halloween shop.
It was early morning, the shop was still closed.
Unlit. Of course it was some mistake.
But the more I looked
the more it looked like me, hanging askew
among Nixon, Freddy Kruger and Nicole.
Painted rubber with dayglow eyes.
I tried to catch my reflection in the window
but all I got was a blur, a grey blur.
When I got too close my breath misted over.
At least it was me breathing.
There was no one around. I could've smashed
the shop window and stolen myself
and run like hell.
Or I could come back when the shop opened
and prove it was some disney character
or no mask at all.
Just early morning at the wrong angle.
The sides of my rubber head caved in
around emptiness, a price tag was stuck behind my ear
like a secretary's pencil.
There I was, dangling from a nail.
It didn't hurt. Really, it didn't hurt.
I touched my forehead on my side of the glass.
No wires and my skin was warm.
I still wasn't sure.

VIEW

A middle-aged man looks out a late night hotel window
at a slow river flowing over the hoods of cars.
A river only he can see.
A river drawing red green traffic light reflections
down among dead leaves, surface algae,
a rotting, half-sunburned branch.
He peers past striped venetian blinds
and curtains clean enough for a funeral home.
The river isn't real except at night.
He's alone in the hotel room
with the lights out behind him.
The night people don't look up
and his face looking down
is not about to interrupt or throw pebbles,
where would he get a pebble?
The cheap hotel room waits politely
for him to go away.
It waits politely for everyone to go away.
A middle-aged man in his shirtsleeves
leans out the hotel window
listening to frogs and the faint echoes of nightjars.
The shimmer of mosquitoes.
The hotel room isn't real either.

COLD WATER

Cold water grinds out of clanking pipes.
I'm glaring at it while bathroom tiles
slap my bare feet.
Finally I splash both hands full of liquid knives
over my sleep-sticky face
and come out gasping blindly for a towel
or a bandage.
Cold water still remembers a stone
where throats were cut to warm it.
No other warmth is acceptable.
Eyes full of water I can see the stone
on the other side. Waiting.
I pay no more attention than to the crumbs of dreams
being washed down the basin.
Soap is *supposed* to hurt my eyes,
I reach for the soap.
The heater's just been fixed and will be fixed again
but it won't do.
Cold water grasps my throat,
remembering.

41

CRYING BABY

A baby's crying suddenly, loudly,
his eyes crunched up,
his face red, his short arms and legs thrash wildly
as if someone stuck a long silver needle
into his round belly.
His mother tries to hush him
but he's forgotten she exists.
All the other cafe noises
disappear down his furious throat.
The canned classical ceiling music, conversations,
even the lurch and grind of the espresso machine
that I'm used to thinking of as loud.
Compared to the baby we're all broken shells
and seaweed and driftwood left behind
on time's beach as the tide goes out;
we're not really real, not like him.
He hurts, he screams, nothing else matters.
Then his mother gives him something
and he stops, just as suddenly.
We all sit in the cafe's comparative silence,
a little shaken, oddly wistful.
We're looking at our own hurts,
the ones we never scream about because we're grown-up,
the ones that never go away.

DRY BONES

About 20. Tanned brown glowing skin,
brown shaggy dog hair,
sprawled in a chair in the cafe
with a big mug of hot brown coffee, a batch of friends
and his brown guitar sprawled lazily by his side.
He's playing with a pile of bones on the table,
dry bones, white bones.
A whole bag of bones I bought at the flea market
to be strung into necklaces, maybe a flute,
maybe just forgotten and gathering dust in a corner.
So much is forgotten.
He piles knobby bone on bone
like a castle of cards about to fall down
under his living hands and his warm breath.
My sister sticks a pink and yellow flower
in the top of the bone castle, swaying like a flag.
His shirt's open. Hot day.
A drop of sweat's caught in curly brown chest hairs.
White bones, dry bones, curved bones we pick up
and stroke wonderingly. And put them down again.
Someone says something and we all laugh,
the castle falls.
Life leaps in his curved brown throat
laughing at ruins. His hands thump the table.
And the bones, they laugh too.
White bones. Dry bones.

AIRPLANE PILOT

Do you read me? Come in, hello, hello.
Please answer.
I am the pilot and you are the air controller.
I want to come closer to you.
Give me directions.
The sky is full of ghosts making static.
I'm flying a lonely engine waiting for directions,
are you out there? Is anyone out there?
The sky is big as god or the absence of god or both.
No one can reach it or reach thru it to each other.
There's clouds blowing under me, mixed with ghosts.
If I try to land will you be there
or is there a mountain? Crash and burn.
Flying blind. We're all flying blind.
Last night I heard you on my radio,
you were asleep, you were dreaming.
There were no words.
I set my compass by the tone of your voice.
I'd have enough fuel if I knew where I was going.
Where are you? Where am I?
The sky hurts between us,
tender as a bruise avoiding touch.
We're all flying lonely engines
wanting to come closer.
Calling to each other, "Are you out there?
Come in, hello, hello."

TREE OF FOOTPRINTS

An old winter tree with muddy footprints
instead of leaves,
brown and blown, a tall tree.
Boots, bare feet, tennis shoes all about to fall
and float down a rainy gutter. Only the prints.
No shoes, no feet, nobody climbs trees
in the middle of a cold winter night
to leave their steps, like hands in wet cement.
And yet. And yet.
No other leaves, no flowers.
And even the footprints are dry,
shriveled with autumn, wrinkled.
Even the brown mud would've turned brown by now.
And if there is a tree of our footsteps, a tall tree
when did we walk there and who with?
Can you tell from the shape of the falling leaves
crumbling between your fingers?

45

THE VAMPIRE LADY

When the vampire lady fell in love
she wished he had no blood.
For the first time in centuries
she remembered being alive and losing her appetite,
writing initials in gravy and privately
feeding the meat to the dog,
hoping her brothers didn't see.
When the vampire lady fell in love
and still heard the blue vein beating in his neck
like a bell she felt cheap.
Surely this was different.
She wanted it to be different.
If the vampire lady wanted to blush in his presence
she had to feed first,
she had to blush with other people's blood;
it was an invasion of privacy.
How dare strangers be needed
to warm her skin for his touch?
They were never alone.
When they finally made love her veins were full
of half-dissolved memories from 4 different people.
She was so busy seeming human
that when he gave her a hickey she nearly fell out of bed.
Afterwards, the vampire lady watched him sleep,
listening to the sounds he made breathing.
No one would mistake her for human.
She left a note saying she'd been called away,
a brother was ill, he would hear from her.
Time passed. When the man's son
was the same age the man had been that night
the vampire lady sought the boy out
with no pretense.
And drained him to the last drop.

PHOTOGRAPH ALBUM

There was a fire in a photograph album.
Only the black and white beach burned,
and the grey circus and the photographed people
tore off clothes burning fierce white
and tried to stomp them out.
Only in the photograph album,
the brown leather album with gilt lettering
lying on a black walnut table.
All the people beating on the sides of their pictures
to get out of the fire,
all those people died long ago.
And not one from fire.
The fire was in the **ph**otograph album,
only in the album.
I won't look at it again.

NEW YEAR'S EVE

So many of last year's memories are in the freezer,
not to be looked at
till they're at the bottom of an ice cube
melting in a strong drink at the end of a party
and the memory doesn't bite our tongues
till we're drunk enough to ignore it.
Not just bad memories, but ones that don't fit.
Time's hiccups.
Something about time.
I'm over half a century old,
I should've learned something about time.
I believe in world war II and god both of which started
before I was born, and in sweet rock candy on a string,
I forget why they took it off the market
but I can still feel how sticky it made my fingers
and half my face.
Each new year is the first year that ever was,
like each love.
No one ever loved before.
And I must believe them all: each year, each love,
any forever that shines against the dark
however briefly.
All our moans and card tricks.
Time is only a question. Answer it.
A child who just dissected grandfather's pocket watch
sits on the floor, surrounded by coils, wheels
and levers, and tries to glue the hands
over his upper lip for a fake mustache.
He is time, chortling with implacable whims.
He puts everything in his mouth.
He puts everyone in his mouth.
Time runs out on a parking meter or a marriage
or a patient who isn't convalescing

in a convalescent home.
Time is famous for standing still
but it hasn't been caught yet.
I should've learned something.
Each season exists on a different planet
all year around, each season breathes always
in a different language.
I value each day because my time is limited,
that's how I know this is not my time.
Each time belongs only to those
who know they'll live forever,
with time to throw away.
I like to watch them wear the trappings of savagery
for protection. Piercings, studs, chains, tattoos,
their own strokable throats.
And yes, I believe them,
as I believe in each year,
each love, god and world war II.
Time can take care of the contradictions.
We hurt each other.
I don't know if we hurt each other more
than we used to,
but we used to be more surprised by it.
We tried to hide it.
Now, when time wears a bloody coat,
that's just the coat he's wearing.
If I were still living forever
with a hook deep in my throat
pulling me up to the sun I'd change everything.
I wouldn't need any help.
I remember.
Time forgets, we are his only memories,
he comes back for bedtime stories

and we tell him mainly what should've happened
and try to believe it ourselves.
Because time slept in my body
time learned more about me
than I learned about him.
But time forgets.
Our breath forgets our mouths.
Our fingerprints change when we have bad dreams.
We're tightrope walkers between the centuries
where dark is a long way down.
Where suicide plums splat on rocks below,
a spreading purple stain with rotting pits.
We are the baby born at midnight.
This time we'll get it right.
This time.

Julia Vinograd is a Berkeley street poet. She has published 41 books of poetry, and won the American Book Award of The Before Columbus Foundation. She received a B.A. from the University of California at Berkeley and an M.F.A. from the University of Iowa.